MOUNTAIN NAVIGATION

by

PETER CLIFF

Foreword by Iain Peter

First Edition 1978
Second Edition 1980
Reprinted 1985
Third Edition 1986
Reprinted 1987
Reprinted 1990
Fourth Edition 1991
Reprinted 1993
Reprinted 1995
Reprinted 1998
Fifth Edition 2002
Sixth Edition 2006

Ordnance Survey maps are reproduced by permission of the Ordnance Survey UK, the Swiss map by permission of Swisstopo Silva, compasses by permission of Silva Compasses (U.K.), and the photograph of the Casio watch was supplied by Facewest Ltd.

The diagrams are by Mike Anderson and the cartoons by Doug Godlington.

Cover photograph: Tarmachen Ridge, Tayside, Scotland.

Cliff, Peter.
Mountain Navigation – 6th Edition
1   Hiking – Great Britain.
2   Mountaineering – Great Britain.
3   Orientation – Great Britain.
4   Title

796.5'22   GV199.44.G7

ISBN 1-871890-55-1

Printed by The Max Design & Print, Clifton Moor, York YO30 4XF

FOREWORD

"Mountain Navigation" is the definitive instructional work for anyone who wants to learn how to navigate in the mountains. Peter Cliff has distilled all of his vast experience at sea, on ski and, most importantly, on foot into an easily understood and concise manual. It is because he writes from such valid experience that this book is so admirably and markedly superior to anything else on the subject.

Learning to navigate is first and foremost practical – you need to spend the time practising on the ground to become familiar with the navigation techniques required to make your way efficiently in the hills. However, you will find that "Mountain Navigation" provides all of the background theory and explanation that are so crucial to good, practical navigation. It is concise, uncomplicated and well illustrated with simple easy to follow diagrams.

The mere fact that the previous editions have sold over 70,000 copies is in itself proof of "Mountain Navigation's" status as *the* reference work on the subject. You will find that an understanding and mastery of its contents can only improve the enjoyment you derive from the time spent exploring the hills and mountains.

Iain Peter   April 2006

Introduction

Map Reading

The Compass

Estimating Time

Estimating Paces

The Altimeter

GPS (Global Positioning System)

Bad Weather Navigation

Alpine Glacier Navigation

If Lost . . .

INTRODUCTION

There seem to be two tendencies in navigation.

The first is to pull out the compass or the GPS at the first opportunity and to rely on them entirely. As will be shown later, both can be unreliable; so it is necessary to have other skills (particularly the ability to read a map), and to use technical devices in conjunction with these skills.

The second tendency is to assume that navigation is a very precise affair - i.e. we either know exactly where we are, or we are lost. But it is seldom as definite as that. In fact, once the basic skills have been mastered, navigation is really about collecting available information and then making an objective and accurate assessment of that information.

Schemes for training and assessing people to instruct and lead others in the mountains attach great importance to navigation, and the skills described in this book will be of particular value to people involved in those schemes.

Another important factor is Mountain Rescue statistics. A very high proportion of mountain accidents is due, directly or indirectly, to bad navigation. Accidents are often reported as being due to exposure, slipping on snow or grass etc. etc. - but in many of these cases the accident would not have happened in the first place if the navigation had been good.

When the weather is fine and the terrain familiar, navigation is a simple matter. But to navigate across unfamiliar mountains in bad weather demands a high degree of proficiency in several skills - one or more of which will be used at any particular time.

This book describes those skills.

MAP READING

Mountain navigation can be thought of in two parts. The first part is map reading: i.e. the ability to look at the map and to be able to picture the ground in your mind. The second part is all the rest and includes the compass, estimating time, estimating paces, the altimeter and GPS.

THE IMPORTANCE OF MAP READING

The first part, map reading, is the vital one. If you are good at this, you will only have to resort to the other skills in difficult conditions. Most of the time you can keep walking at a steady pace, having occasional quick looks at the map without breaking your step.

If you are on your own, there is nothing more pleasant than stopping whenever you want to look at the view or the map. But if you are the leader of a group, continual stops by you make life difficult for the rest of the group (particularly those at the back). They won't thank you for it, and they'll probably begin to wonder if you know where you are.

The ability to move at a steady pace while navigating over unfamiliar ground is the essence of mountain navigation; and if you master the first part, map reading, you are most of the way there.

CONVENTIONAL SIGNS

The symbols used on maps are called conventional signs. It is unnecessary to learn them all parrot-fashion, as every map has them shown as a legend, which will be on the side or the bottom of the map.

As a mountaineer, I have not yet found it necessary to be able to distinguish between a church with a tower, one with a spire, or one with neither. On the other hand, if you are out in bad visibility and the map shows outcrops and cliffs in front of you, it is obviously important to know whether, if you keep walking, you will be at the top or the bottom of them. The symbols used by the Ordnance Survey for outcrops and cliffs are rather confusing, as illustrated over the page.

Cliffs are shown with the continuous line at the top, while outcrops are shown with it at the bottom.

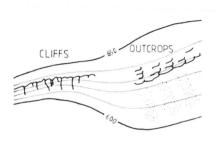

Fig.1. Outcrops and cliffs.

"– COULD HAVE SWORN IT WAS A CLIFF – MUST HAVE BEEN AN OUTCROP!"

GRID REFERENCES

British maps are covered with grid lines, lines running north/ south and west/east on the map. Each line is numbered, and the squares formed by these lines are one kilometre squares. A system of four-figure, six-figure and eight-figure references is used to pinpoint positions.

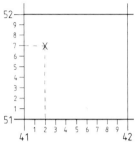

To get the six-figure reference, the sides of the squares are split into tenths, using the ruler part of your compass. This gives the 3rd and 6th figures. In Fig.2, point X is at 41**25**17.

Fig.2. Six-figure grid reference.

You always take the figures along the bottom first, and then go up the side. To help remember this: "You go in the door and along the hall, before going up the stairs".

If you use a compass with a romer, working out grid references is quick and easy.

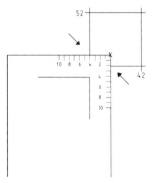

1. Place the corner of the relevant romer on the point, as shown in Fig.3.

2. Read off the figures on the romer, as shown by the arrows in the diagram. In this case we get 41**45**12.

Fig. 3. Using a romer for grid references.

Just as a four-figure reference covers a square (a one kilometre square), so a six-figure one gives a 100 metre square. Your point could be anywhere within that 100 metre square.

SCALE

The scale of the map is the relationship between the distance on the map and the distance on the ground. 1:50,000 is a scale found on maps all round the world, and it means that 1 centimetre on the map equals 50,000 centimetres on the ground. 50,000 centimetres is 500 metres.

Fig.(4). Photograph of Loganlea Reservoir.

In the photograph above, a house called 'The Howe' is shown in the bottom left-hand corner. If you were to walk from there along the far side of the reservoir, after 600 metres you would come to a stream, and after another 400 metres you would come to the end of the reservoir - a total distance of one kilometre.

Note that the trees showing in the photograph around 'The Howe' are not on the map. They must have grown since the map was surveyed, and the presence or absence of trees is the most common cause of differences between maps and actual terrain.

Using a compass or ruler, measure the distance on the map Fig.5 between 'The Howe' and the end of the reservoir. You will find it is 2 centimetres.

On this map, therefore, 2 centimetres equals 1 kilometre on the ground. 1 centimetre is therefore 500 metres ground (which is 50,000 centimetres).

This map has a scale of 1:50,000.

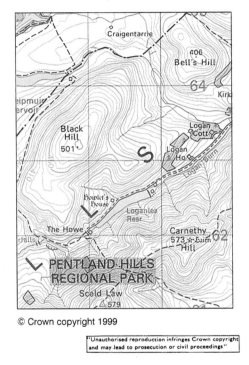

© Crown copyright 1999

"Unauthorised reproduction infringes Crown copyright and may lead to prosecution or civil proceedings"

Fig.5. Map of area in Fig.4.

On the 1:50,000 scale one kilometre round is shown by 2 centimetres on the map. If you want more detail, some areas are covered by the 1:25,000 scale, where a kilometre on the ground is represented by four centimetres on the map - i.e. you get double the detail.

Figs.6 and 7 on the next page show the same area on both scales.

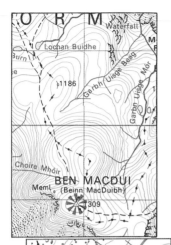

Fig.6   1:50,000

The two maps show exactly the same area, although on different scales.

Fig.7.   1:25,000

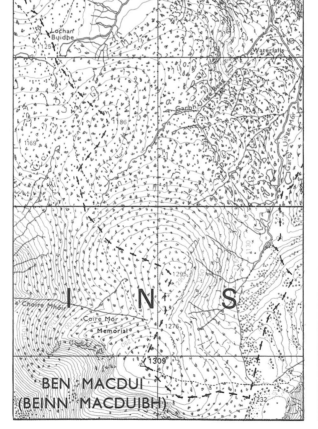

One of the advantages of the 1:50,000 over the 1:25,000 is that the 1:50,000 gives a much clearer overall picture. Looking at the 1:50,000, the general shape of the mountain stands out clearly. In comparison, the general picture on the 1:25,000 tends to be obscured by the mass of detail - particularly the little dots marking all the boulders. This is because the contour line, which is a very important symbol for the mountaineer, does not stand out on the 1:25,000 as well as it does on the 1:50,000.

The good point about the 1:25,000, on the other hand, is that every small feature is marked. Look at the extra detail on the streams and lochans - they are shown in far greater detail than on the 1:50,000.

Perhaps the most difficult thing to get used if using both maps is the relationship between the density of the contour lines and the steepness of the ground. Look for a moment at the maps, particularly at the slope running north from Ben Macdui down to Garbh Uisge Beag. If used to the density as shown on the 1:50,000, one might well underestimate the steepness of the slope when going over to the 1:25,000.

Most walkers and mountaineers will use both the Landranger 1:50,000 and the Explorer 1:25,000 - the Landranger being excellent for general use and the Exporer having that useful extra detail, essential for bad weather navigation.

INTERPETING THE MAP

The most important part of navigation is to look at the map and to be able to picture the actual ground in your mind. This pictorial image is created by the contour line - a line on the map joining points of equal height. They are coloured brown; every fifth one is shaded heavier; and at regular intervals the heights are given.

The shape of the contour lines show the shape of the hillside; and the spacing between them or density shows the steepness of the hillside.

On the 1:50,000 Landranger the vertical interval between each contour line is 10 metres. On the 1:25,000 Explorer it is 5 metres in lowland areas and 10 metres in upland or highland areas, so it is essential to check in the legend to see which it is. If you go abroad you will find different intervals, for example 20 metres is used on the Swiss 1:50,000 maps. One of the first things to do when you open a new map is to check the contour interval and you will find this written down somewhere, usually in the legend which describes the symbols used. Whatever interval is used, it will be the same for the whole of the map, with one notable exception - the French 1:25,000 maps use10 metres for everything French and 20 metres for anything over the border.

With practice, while looking at the map a pictorial image or photograph comes up in your mind. Once you can do this, you will be able to navigate accurately.

Fig.(9) shows a photograph of a hill and Fig.(10) shows the map of   the same area. The photograph was taken from the top of Scald Law, looking towards Carnethy Hill. If you look closely at the map you can identify the shape and steepness of Carnethy Hill.

For example, the south ridge of Carnethy Hill has contour lines fairly close together all the way except for one section near the top where they are more spaced out (a more level section), followed by four close together near the top (a steeper section). This level section and the final steeper section can be seen clearly on the photograph - the right-hand skyline.

Fig.9. Photograph of Carnethy Hill

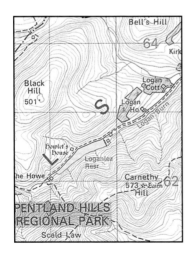

Fig. 10. Map of Carnethy Hill. Landranger 1:50,000

© Crown copyright 1999

Figs. 11 to 16 show on the left-hand side the map of various typical mountain features, and on the right-hand side they are shown in elevation.

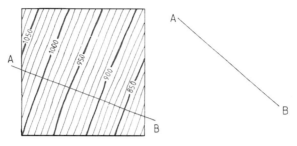

Fig. 11. An even slope.

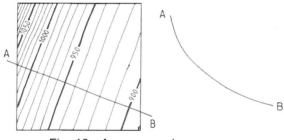

Fig. 12. A concave slope.

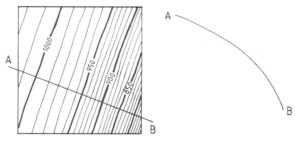

Fig.13. A convex slope.

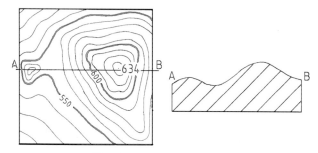

Fig.14. A double top.

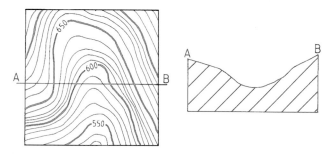

Fig.15. A valley.

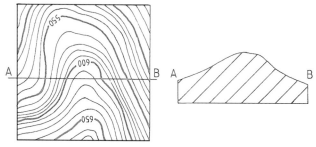

Fig. 16. A spur or ridge.

The most obvious difference between the maps in Figs. 15 and 16 is that in Fig.16 the figures indicating the contour lines are upside down, whereas in Fig.15 they are the right way up. This is intentional; and it gives an immediate indication of whether the slope goes up or down. If, when you look at the map, the figures are the correct way up, then the low ground is towards the bottom of the map and the high is towards the top. Conversely, if the figures are upside down, high ground is towards the bottom of the map and low is towards the top. In other words, to quickly tell whether the ground is going up or down, look to see which way up the writing is.

If you become good at interpreting the map and at picturing the actual ground in your mind, you will be able to anticipate the ground and select the best route.

1. Anticipation: to anticipate what is coming in terms of features is the nitty gritty of navigation. With this anticipation you know what is coming next–e.g. a short steep slope, or a flat section, or a stream, or a descending traverse etc., etc,–and as things appear when expected, you know where you are. If they do not appear when expected, stop and have a look at the map; work out where you went wrong; and, if necessary, read the chapter "If Lost…" !

2. Route Choice: in selecting the best route on a particular day, you will need to weigh up many factors, not least the experience of the party, the weather and the conditions under foot. If you are good at interpreting the map, certain choices will be obvious, for example:

i. keeping off ridges in high wind.

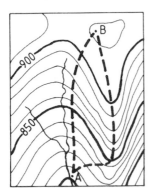

Fig.17.

In Fig.17 there are two routes from A to B. One is up the ridge on the right; the other up the stream to the col, and then to B. In high winds the ridge could be dangerous, particularly in a gusting wind which is usual in Britain, and it would certainly be tiring. A more comfortable and safe route would be up the stream.

ii. keeping to ridges in heather and snow. Heather usually grows thickest in the protected valley floor, and snow is blown into the valley floors. The exposed ridges therefore usually offer better conditions underfoot for walking.

iii. avoiding dangerous slopes in avalanche conditions. The most common avalanche in this country is the windslab, which forms on lee slopes. If you are going to an area in winter, find out what the weather conditions (particularly wind) have been. If for example, there has been a strong SE wind, avoid slopes facing NW.

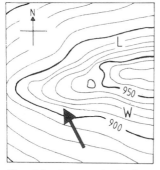

In Fig.18 a SE wind would blow in the direction of the arrow. The NW slope becomes a lee slope (L) and is therefore suspect. The windward (w) slope is normally safer.

Fig. 18. Lee and windward slopes.

In Fig.19, to descend from A to B in snow conditions, where windslab is suspected, there are four possibilities:

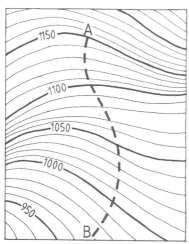

i. the slope on the left as we look at it is dangerous because it is convex, particularly at 1050m. - point of greatest tension.

ii. the direct line A to B is a uniform angle of slope and is safer than the convex.

iii. the slope on the right as we look at it is concave and is usually safest, but there could be windslab on the top steep bit.

iv. the dotted line is a compromise, taking the safest of each slope and avoiding the worst.

Fig.19. Safest route on a snow slope.

13

THE COMPASS

TYPES OF COMPASS

The best type of compass for hillwalkers and mountaineers is the orienteering type as produced by Silva, Suunto and Recta. They are light, simple, and they do everything necessary. There is a wide choice available, some more suited to orienteering and some better for the mountaineer. These are the features to look for:

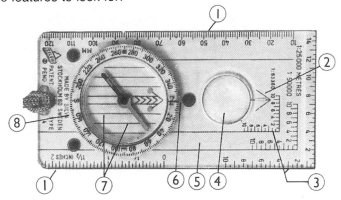

Fig.20. Silva Type 4 compass with romer.

1. Scales. 2. Direction of travel arrow. 3. Romer. 4. Magnifying lense. 5.Transparent baseplate. 6. Read bearings here. 7. Orienting lines in compass housing. 8. Degrees dial in 2° calibrations.

- A romer is invaluable for measuring distances quickly.

- Compass housing baseplates may be solid or transparent, and for lining up on grid lines, the transparent one is easier.

- The degrees may be on the side or on the top of the compass housing. When on top, they are easier to read.

- Some compasses have available scales to slip over the front of the compass. These tend to get lost, are fiddly, and are not therefore recommended.

- Baseplates with rubber feet do not slide around on the map and so are a good idea.

- Luminous points make night navigation much easier, and although you may not be planning a night trip, it might come along unexpectedly.

- A magnifying glass in the baseplate is useful for looking closely at contour lines, for removing splinters etc.

- Most compasses have the degree calibrations in 2° while some more expensive ones have them in ½°. In mountain navigation, errors with compass bearings inevitably occur (see later) and it can be argued that, by having ½° calibrations, we reduce that error, but I think it is very difficult to operate with that degree of precision and personally find that 2° works fine.

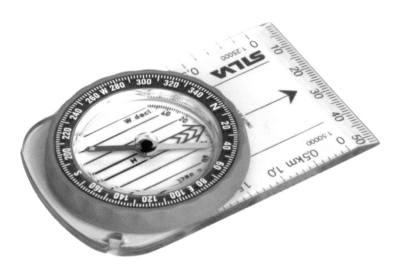

Fig 21. Silva Field 7 Compass

A good basic compass with 1:50,000 and 1:25,000 scales.

USES OF THE COMPASS

The compass is a very versatile instrument and can be used for:

1. measuring distances on the map.
2. working out grid references.
3. finding north.
4. setting the map.
5. calculating bearings, map to compass, for following.
6. calculating bearings, compass to map, for:
     i.   identifying peaks etc.
     ii. resections (cocked hats).
     iii. single back bearing with a known feature.
     iv. aspects of slope.

1. MEASURING DISTANCES ON THE MAP.

If you have a compass with a romer, measuring distances, particularly those up to one kilometre, is very easy, as on both the 1:25,000 and 1:50,000 scales one calibration equals 100 metres. If you don't have a romer, you use the ruler on the compass, and this is where mistakes occur.

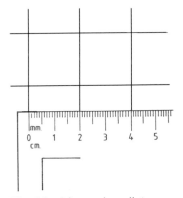

On the 1:50,000

2 cms. equal 1 kilometre.
1 cm. equals 500 metres.
1 mm equals 50 metres.

The problem is that people often expect 1 mm. to equal 100 metres.

Fig. 22. Measuring distances on the 1:50,000 map using the scale or ruler of the compass.

On the 1:25,000, 4 centimetres equal 1 kilometre, and 1 millimetre equals 25 metres.

It is just a matter of familiarisation and practice; but it seems that this basic step causes a lot of errors and it cannot therefore be as easy as it appears. To cut out this potential source of error, the answer is simple: buy a compass with a romer.

2. WORKING OUT GRID REFERENCES.

Again, if you have a romer this is easy - see Fig. 3 on page 3. If you don't have a romer, it means using the ruler on the compass to split the kilometre square into tenths.

1:50,000   on the millimetre/centimetre ruler there are 2 calibrations (millimetres) for every tenth - see Fig. 22.

1:25,000   more complicated, as on the millimetre/centimetre scale there are 4 calibrations to a tenth.

3. FINDING NORTH.

If you ask someone what the main use of a compass is, the answer will probably be to find North. But in itself this is not a great help, unless you happen to be on the way to the North Pole.

"...UNLESS YOU HAPPEN TO BE
ON YOUR WAY TO THE NORTH POLE".

There are in fact three norths in navigation - True, Grid and Magnetic.

True North: where the North Pole is and almost the same as Grid North. For mountain navigation purposes it can be ignored.

Grid North: the north to which the grid lines on the map point.

Magnetic North: because of the Earth's magnetism, the needle of the compass is pulled over to one side. In Britain it is pulled 3° - 4° to the west and this is reducing by about 12' a year.

Magnetic variation varies from place to place, and from year to year. On the map, among the conventional signs, the difference between Grid and Magnetic North will be shown.

For example: "Magnetic north is estimated at 4°26' west of grid north for July 2001. Annual change is approximately 12' east."

If you lose your compass, you can find north by other methods. For interest's sake here are the two most well known ones, although neither are accurate.

By watch and sun:

– hold the watch flat in your hand.

– point the hour hand at the sun (ignore the minute hand).

– bisect the angle between 12 o'clock and the hour hand, and this points SOUTH.

– of course most of us now use digital watches and this won't work, but maybe it bleeps when pointing north.

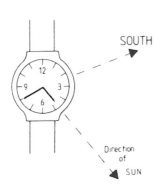

Fig.23. Finding north by watch and sun.

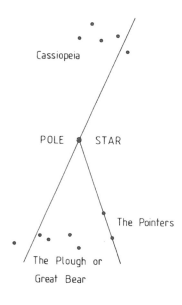

Cassiopeia

POLE ★ STAR

The Pointers

The Plough or
Great Bear

*Fig. 24. Finding north
by the stars.*

By the stars:

– the Plough revolves round the Pole Star, but, wherever it is, its pointers point to the Pole Star.

– Cassiopeia is the same distance on the other side of the Pole Star, shaped like a flat W or M.

4 SETTING THE MAP

This means getting the top of the map pointing north, so that the features on the map coincide with those on the ground. If you are facing south, it will mean the writing on the map is upside-down.

There are two ways of setting the map:

(a) **By Landmarks** If you know where you are and can recognise landmarks, line up the landmarks on the map with those on the ground. This will result in the top of the map pointing north.

(b) **By Compass**–hold the compass flat, so that the magnetic needle points steadily north.

–line up the map underneath the compass, with the grid lines parallel to the magnetic needle.

–the map is now pointing north.

–for practical purposes magnetic variation can be ignored.

When the map is correctly set, identify on the map the position you are at. If it shows on the map that there are, for example, crags high up the slope on the right, then a look at the slope on the right will show they are there. Setting the map means you can pick out from the map any features, and by looking in that direction you can identify them on the ground.

BEARINGS, MAP TO COMPASS

This is the more usual use of the compass. If you want to travel in bad visibility, take the bearing from the map, put it onto the compass, and then follow the compass. In the first part, measuring the bearing on the map, the compass is being used as a protractor.

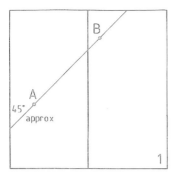

The steps are:

1. hold the map flat–
it doesn't matter which
way it is pointing.
Estimate the bearing by
eye - this avoids getting
it 180° wrong. In the
example, it is about 45°
when going from A to B.

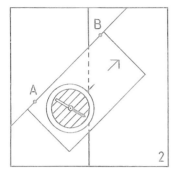

2. place one long edge
of the compass along the
imaginary line AB, with
the direction of travel
arrow pointing the way
you want to go.

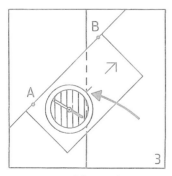

3. turn the compass
housing until the
orienting lines in the
compass housing are
parallel to the grid lines
on the map. Read off the
bearing at the point
marked by the arrow.
This is the grid bearing.

*Fig. 25. Measuring a
bearing on the map.*

4. Because the magnetic needle is pulled off to one side,
we must allow for this by adding or subtracting the relevant
magnetic variation. In Britain and the rest of Europe it is always
added; but in some parts of the world it is subtracted. To
remember to add it in Britain, here are three aids:

i. Add for mag., get rid for grid.
ii. Grid unto magnetic, Add - GUMA.
   Magnetic unto grid, subtract - MUGS.
iii. The landscape is bigger than the map, therefore the bearing for the landscape (magnetic) should be bigger than that for the map (grid).

In this case we have a grid bearing, so we add the magnetic variation (Add for mag) to make it magnetic. If the grid bearing for example is 50°and the magnetic variation is 4° the magnetic bearing is 54° . Turn the compass housing until you have this on the compass.

5. In order to follow the compass, hold it flat in your hand in front of you. Now turn round until the red end of the magnetic needle points to North on the compass housing and is parallel to the orienting lines.

It is now correctly aligned.

The direction in which to go is shown by the Direction of Travel Arrow.

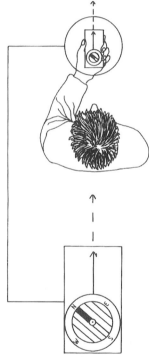

Fig. 26. Aligning the compass.

Deviation. When aligning the compass, be very careful that there is no metal near you as it will affect the needle of the compass. Such things as ice axes, watches, tins of food, karabiners etc. may affect it to a significant degree - as do certain rocks, e.g. the Cuillins of Skye.

ERRORS WHEN TAKING BEARINGS, MAP TO COMPASS

Imagine you are out on a mountain; it is windy, cold and snowing. You are trying to take off a bearing with cold fingers and two pairs of gloves on. Errors may occur in the following places:

i.   when taking the bearing off the map.
ii. when adding the magnetic variation.
iii. when following the bearing.

In stages (i) and (ii) an error of 4°- 6° is not unusual. In trying to follow the bearing a further error of 4°- 6° must be allowed for. If these errors are cumulative, you have an error of 8°- 12°.

A 6°error means that, on a leg of 500 metres, you are 52 metres out.

A 12°error means that, on a leg of 500 metres, you are 104 metres out.

The percentage on a 6°error is just over 10%: and on a 12° error it is just over 20%.

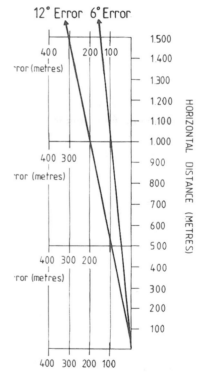

Fig.27. Effect of 6°and 12° errors on a compass bearing.

BEARINGS, COMPASS TO MAP

There are four occasions when you might want to take a bearing with your compass and convert it to the map:

1. in order to identify a peak etc.
2. to work out your position through a resection (known as a Cocked Hat).
3. to combine a single bearing with a known feature.
4. to take the aspect of the slope in order to work out your position.

1. In order to identify a peak etc. You might be able to identify it by setting the map and seeing what's there; but if this is not accurate enough, use the compass as follows:

i.   holding the compass flat, point the direction of travel arrow at the peak.
ii. turn the compass housing until the orienting arrow in the housing lies underneath the magnetic needle and the red end of the magnetic needle points to North on the housing.
iii. read off the bearing.
iv. subtract magnetic variation to get the grid bearing ("get rid for grid").
v.   lay the compass on the map - it doesn't matter which way the map is pointing, because you are now using the compass as a protractor - with one of the long sides on the point you are at (Point A in Fig.28) and with the orienting lines in the compass housing parallel to the grid lines on the map, and the orienting arrow pointing to North.

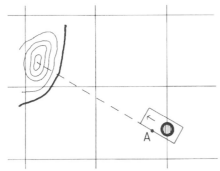

Somewhere along the side of the compass, and continuation of that line, is the peak - dotted line in Fig.28.

Fig.28. Identifying an object.

2. Resections (also known as Cocked Hats). While the use of resections or back bearings to make 'Cocked Hats' is useful when, for example, sailing along the coast in a boat, it is a vastly overrated skill in mountain navigation. This is because, if you are lost, it is unlikely that you will be able to positively identify the two or three points necessary to do one. For interest, these are the steps in making a resection.

i. select at least two, and preferably three, points which you can positively identify and which are at widely different angles from you.

ii. with the first point go through steps i – iv of 'In order to identify a peak' - i.e. take its bearing and convert to grid.

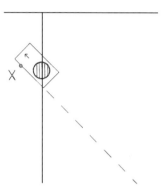

iii. put on long side of the compass on the point (X in Fig. 29) with the orienting lines parallel to the grid lines, and the orienting arrow pointing north on the map.

iv. you are somewhere along the side of the compass and the extension of that line.

Fig. 29. Resection.

v. repeat with the other two points (Points Z and Y in Fig. 30). A 'Cocked Hat' is formed, with your position somewhere inside it.

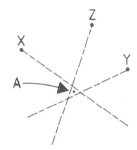

vi. when pinpointing your position within the Cocked Hat, consider the accuracy of your bearings - move your position towards those you felt were good and away from those which were not so good.

Fig. 30. A full resection.

There is a second method of making a resection through backbearings. Take the bearing of the first point and convert to grid (say 280° in Fig. 31). Subtract 180° to get a back bearing of 100°. If you cannot subtract 180°, then add it (e.g. the backbearing of 20° is 200°). Now lay the compass on the map as in Fig. 31 with a bearing of 100°, with the orienting lines parallel to the grid lines, and with the orienting arrow pointing to north on the map.

You will be somewhere along the side of the compass and the extension of that line. Repeat with the other two points for a Cocked Hat.

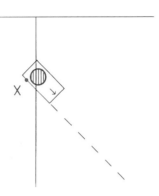

Fig. 31. Backbearing.

This second method could be said to be a purer and safer method, as the bearing is from the known point, and the direction of travel arrow is pointing to where you are. In practice, however, the first method is obviously quicker as there are less stages involved. Since there are less stages, there is less chance of making a mistake.

3. Single backbearing with a known feature. The situation can arise where your approximate position is already defined by an obvious physical feature (e.g. you are following a ridge, a stream, a glacier, the edge of a forest etc.).

Presume you are on the crest of a ridge, as in Fig. 32, but you are not sure how far along it you are. The cloud suddenly lifts for a few seconds and you see a stream junction on your left. Take a bearing on it, and you can put your position at A.

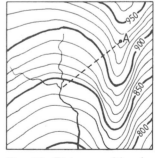

Fig. 32. Fixing position by backbearing and feature.

3. Aspect of Slope. A clear understanding of Aspect of Slope will help you greatly, not only to follow the intended route, but also to extract yourself when you are off route - maybe even lost !

The aspect of a particular slope is the direction it faces.

In Fig. 33 the slope AB has an aspect of roughly 330° .

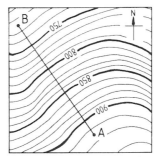

Fig. 33. Aspect of slope.

Imagine you have been out for some time in really bad visibility, and that you are descending a slope which has dangerous outcrops on it. Suppose you are not certain where you are on the slope, and you want to be sure you are not going to walk over the outcrops. All you can see is the slope you are on, and you can't even see much of that. Take the aspect of the slope by:

i. point the compass down the slope and read the bearing. Convert to grid.

ii. put the compass on the map. Keeping the orienting lines in the compass housing parallel with the grid lines on the map, and keeping the orienting arrow pointing north on the map, slide the compass along your presumed route.

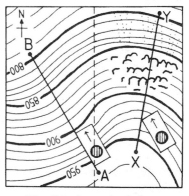

Fig. 34. Aspect of slope.

iii. watch the long side of the compass. When it crosses the contour lines at right angles, this is the slope you are on. In Fig. 34 you are on AB and not XY.

Another application of taking the aspect of a slope is where you take the bearing off in advance to ensure that you set off down the right slope.

Fig. 35. Aspect of slope.

Presume that in Fig. 35 you want to descend from A to C. The obvious danger is turning right too soon and dropping off over the cliffs and outcrops. To avoid this, go to B first (compass bearing and estimate of distance by timing or pacing); and then descend the slope BC.

But before you set off from A, work out the aspect of BC (roughly 320°), and put this bearing as a magnetic bearing on a second compass.

When you think you are at B, point the second compass straight down the slope. If the magnetic needle lines up directly above the orienting arrow, then you are on slope BC.

We take this concept 'Aspect of Slope' a bit further in the chapter 'If Lost ....'

PROBLEMS WITH COMPASSES

Deviation. As already mentioned, be very careful to keep things like ice axes, watches, tins of food, karabiners etc. well away from the compass. They may affect the needle dramatically.

Bubbles. With any fluid filled compass air bubbles may form. It may occur over 1,000 metres in altitude and is due to the drop in atmospheric pressure. Low temperatures contribute to them forming and can be the cause of them forming below that altitude.

The bubbles will disappear when you drop back below that altitude and when the temperature returns to normal.

Reversed polarity. The magnetic needle of the compass may be affected by a magnet or by the magnetic fields which exist around such things as electrical circuits, knives, scissors or any ferrous object. The polarity of the needle may be partially reversed, in which case the needle becomes slow to move and slow to settle; or it may be completely reversed, in which case the magnetic (North) needle points south.

To get rid of reversed polarity, quickly stroke the south pole of a strong magnet outwards along the North end of the needle; and then check it against a compass known to be correct.

ESTIMATING TIME

'Estimating Time' can be thought of in two degrees of accuracy: general and detailed.

By general I mean the ability to plan a route for the time available bearing in mind the strength of the party, the weather and the conditions underfoot. You think in terms of half-hours, and probably keep an open mind as to the exact route until you actually get out there on the mountain.

By detailed I mean the ability to estimate a section to within minutes, to an accuracy of 10%. So if you estimate a particular section to take half-an-hour, you should arrive within three minutes either side.

Few would disagree with the good sense of the first one, the general accuracy. As to the second one, the detailed accuracy, this has the following advantages.

• It helps your general accuracy.
• In bad visibility it gives you an essential dimension, because it tells you how far you have gone. When combined with accurate compass work and map reading, it means you can navigate in bad conditions.

The traditional way of estimating time is Naismith's Rule, but as we will shortly see there is a drawback with this system, and I will therefore start by describing the system which I use, which is simple and quick.

A SIMPLE SYSTEM

Looking at the map decide whether the ground is basically flattish or uphill. The exercise using Fig. 37 indicates the difference between the two. If the ground is basically flattish, use the Horizontal method; and if it is uphill, use the Vertical method.

Horizontal Method

Over flat ground or ground which slopes gently downhill, it may be possible to keep up a brisk walking pace of 5 kph. If you are carrying a heavy load or if the going is bad, this will drop to 4 kph or less.

Over undulating ground or ground which goes gently uphill, 4 kph may be the maximum speed; and again it will drop with a heavy load or bad going. One day you might walk a section on hard snow at 5 kph and find on the next day in soft snow you can only manage 2 kph.

So it is a question of judgement, of assessing certain variables. The variables to take into account are:

· Fitness of the party.
· Experience of the party.
· Loads carried - light day sacs as against big ones with tents, weighing 30 kgs or more.
· Conditions underfoot - deep heather as against a ridge or path; deep snow as against hard snow.
· Weather conditions - a strong wind behind or against you.

Always be prepared to change your estimate. For example, if you find the snow has changed from breakable crust to hard windslab, you will move much faster. If someone stops to fasten a jacket, don't forget to add that time to your estimate.

Small ascents and descents can be allowed for, as long as they are gentle.

To make life even easier, you can use a Timing Chart and save yourself having to make any calculations at all. The chart can be written on the back of a map, or carried on a separate card.

Using a Timing Chart is quick and easy; and it saves having to work things out in difficult conditions when a mistake is easily made.

Metres	K.P.H.			
	5	4	3	2
1000	12	15	20	30
800	10	12	16	24
700	9	11	14	21
500	6	7½	10	15
400	5	6	8	12
200	2½	3	4	6
100	1¼	1½	2	3

Fig. 36. Timing Chart.

31

Vertical Method

When the ground has any amount of vertical ascent in it, greater accuracy can be obtained by discarding the horizontal system in favour of one based purely on the vertical ascent. So you ignore the horizontal distance and work only off the vertical height gain. A fit party with good conditions will climb about 500 metres in an hour; but this can easily be reduced to 300 metres in an hour, and this is more like the average.

Greater accuracy can be obtained by making an allowance per contour line. Supposing the vertical interval between contour lines is 10 metres, one minute per contour line is equivalent to 600 metres an hour and is very fast; and 1¼ - 1½ minutes per contour line is more like the average.

The usual variables must be taken into account - e.g. fitness of the party, experience, loads carried, conditions underfoot and weather conditions. In addition it is important to look very closely at the spacing between the contour lines in order to estimate the steepness, as it takes longer to gain a given vertical height on a gentle slope than it does on a steep slope. The steeper the slope, the faster you will climb it.

When counting contour lines, count every fifth line as this is shaded heavier; and then count the individual ones at either end. This is quicker than counting every single line.

Taking the example below, assume that you are going from Lochan Buidhe to Ben Macdui via the subsidiary NE summit. It is summer, the conditions underfoot are good, there is little wind, and you have a light rucsack.

1. From the S end of Lochan Buidhe to Point (1) the path goes gently uphill for 400 metres crossing 4 contour lines. This kind of gentle slope falls between the two systems. On horizontal distance 4 kph gives an estimate of 6 minutes; and on vertical height an allowance of 1½ minutes per contour line for 4 lines also gives an estimate of 6 minutes.

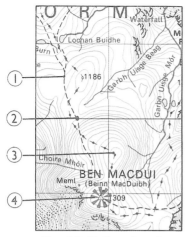

Fig. 37. Estimating time.

(2).From Pt. (1) to Pt. (2) there is a fairly flat section of 600 horizontal metres crossing only one contour line. This is an obvious one for horizontal distance only: 600 metres at, say, 4½ kph gives an estimate of 8¼ minutes.

(3).From Pt. (2) the path goes more steeply to the subsidiary summit Pt. (3). This kind of steepness is good for the vertical height system: 12 contour lines at, say, 1¼ minutes per line gives an estimate of 15 minutes.

4. From there to the summit the path goes gently downhill for 300 metres and then gently uphill for 300 metres. You would probably do 5 kph on the downhill section and 4 kph on the uphill. This could be averaged out at 4½ kph overall, so: 600 metres at 4½ kph gives an estimate of 8¼ minutes.

Descent of Steep Ground

It never seems to be so important to estimate time when going downhill. Maybe it is because there will probably be a clearly defined feature to help the navigation. On gently descending ground use the horizontal timing chart, anything between 4 – 5 kph reducing to 3 kph as the ground steepens. As it steepens even more, so will the rate of descent decrease as you slow up to pick your way down.

NAISMITH'S RULE

This is the traditional rule for estimating time and is: 5 kph + ½ hour for every 300 metres. Be careful to take into account every ascent and descent. For example, if you climb 100 metres, descend 50 metres and finally climb another 70 metres, the overall difference is an ascent of 120 metres, but the estimate must be worked out on 170 metres, since this is the amount actually climbed.

You may find that for much of the time in Britain, 4 kph + ½ hour per 300 metres is accurate. The ½ hour per 300 metres can be expressed as 1 minute per contour line (provided the contour interval is 10 metres), and this makes the arithmetic slightly easier.

The usual variables must be taken into account and the estimate adjusted accordingly, namely: fitness and experience of the party, loads carried, conditions underfoot and weather conditions.

The big disadvantage of Naismith's Rule is that two calculations have to be made - one for the horizontal element and one for the vertical, and then the two have to be added. This is easy enough in a nice warm room, or indeed on a nice warm mountainside; but with a strong wind, temperatures below zero and companions relying on you to get them home, even simple calculations can become surprisingly difficult.

CONCLUSION

Without practice your estimates of time will be more of a hindrance than a help. It does take time to get good at it, but after 5 days or so of concentrated practice you should be getting 10% accuracy on your estimates, and that is good enough to give you an added dimension to use when the conditions are poor and the navigation difficult.

The estimate of time tells you how far along the compass course you are.

If you try the system I recommend, the most important thing is deciding whether a given section of ground falls into the horizontal method or into the vertical method. If a section falls between the two, work it out for both methods - the answer will probably be the same.

If, when you set off on a section you find that one of the variables is not as you anticipated, don't hesitate to alter your estimate. After all, it is supposed to be an aid to your navigation and not some rigid binding rule.

EXERCISES ON ESTIMATING TIME

Using any of the suggested formulas, work out estimated times for the following examples, presuming a small group of fit adults with light rucsacks.

To develop a feel for whether a section falls under the horizontal or vertical method, you might find it useful to do these exercises in conjunction with a map - any map. For example, No.1 is a horizontal distance of 1400 metres with a height gain of 140 metres. Find a slope on your map which is roughly equivalent, and you will see that it is a gently rising gradient.

Under Naismith's Rule the estimate is 32 minutes. Reduce that for the fitness of the party to 29 minutes, and that is what it actually took. On the horizontal distance method it is a gently rising slope; so 1,400 metres at, say, 3 kph gives 28 minutes. On the vertical height method there are 14 contour lines which are well spaced out, being a gently rising slope - so 2 minutes per contour line gives 29 minutes.

No	Distance (metres)	Height+ (metres)	Terrrain	Visibility	Estimated Time	Actual Time
1	1405	+140	Good	Good	32	29
2	1185	-45+75	Good	Good		
3	1610	-330	Boulders	Good		
4	1610	+75	Good	Bad		
5	1205	+150	Boulders	Good		
6	700	+45	Heather	Good		
7	1205	-75	Good	Bad		
8	900	-75	Good	Good		
9	900	+45	Good	Good		
10	1700	+30	8" snow	Good		
11	900	+75	8" snow	Mod.		
12	1205	Nil	snow & rocks	Good		
13	Returning in steps made in No 12					
14	805	+30	Good	Good		
15	1205	+215	Good	Good		
15	590	+140	Good	Good		
17	1005	+335	Good	Good		
18	805	-150	Icy	Good		
19	590	-140	Good	Good		

The actual times taken are on page 37.

ESTIMATING PACES

If you are navigating in very difficult conditions, for example a very dark night or a bad white-out, it is essential to move from one known point to another, keeping the legs short - preferably not more than 400 metres and certainly not more than a kilometre. In this situation, the ability to judge distance travelled by the number of paces taken can be a useful aid. Combined with an estimate of time, you will know how far along the compass course you have gone.

When ascending or descending steep ground it is not worth doing, as the inevitable zig-zags make it inaccurate. But over flattish, undulating ground it can be very accurate - again, with practice. Some people, particularly orienteers, develop this skill to a very high degree, to the extent that they can estimate paces for any kind of terrain and they rely on this rather than on estimating time.

The first thing to do is to try yourself out over a measured distance, say 100 metres. An average figure for a man over flat good going is 130 paces - i.e. 65 double paces. Counting double paces instead of single means half the amount of counting is necessary, which makes the arithmetic easier. Once you have established what you do over flat good going, the next thing is to learn how to adapt for differences in gradient and conditions underfoot. You might find that it is something along these lines:

	Conditions underfoot		
	good	moderate	poor
flat	65	69	80
uphill	78	85	100
downhill	73	75	84

Fig. 38. Double paces per 100 metres.

Those figures are only offered as an example. Everyone takes a different stride and walks differently, but the tendency will be the same - to take more paces as the gradient and going get harder.

When you set off on a leg, it may be difficult to know what the terrain is going to be like. So, rather than estimating paces for the whole leg, start off with the first 100 metres only and work it up in 100 metre sections. For example, presume that you are setting off on a leg which is 800 metres long, and that at the start it looks like being the sort of terrain over which you might do 70 double paces to the 100 metres. You could say '800 metres @ 70 equals a total of 560 double paces', and then off you go counting up to 560. There are two drawbacks doing it this way: firstly, it involves a lot of counting and one can lose count; but more importantly it is difficult to adjust as you come across unexpected differences in terrain. On the other hand, if you take just 100 metres at a time, you can avoid both these problems.

Silva produce a Tachometer, which is useful for counting the 100 legs.

It goes up to 10, and it is easily fixed to the side of the compass by drilling a small hole and gluing.

Fig. 39. A Tachometer.

Alternatively, a handful of small pebbles will do the job.

Practice.   Unless you practice, you will not have the confidence to use this technique; but on the other hand, if you do practice, it means that when the situation arises you have another technique to help your navigation.

I am not suggesting we should go round counting paces the whole time. The occasions when this technique might be used are infrequent - but they are also difficult and serious.

Answers to the exercise on Estimating Time (page 35).

1.29	2.20	3.30	4.36	5.18	6.16	7.26
8.16	9.20	10.37	11.20	12.40	13.30	14.14
15.35	16.20	17.30	18.17	19.10		

THE ALTIMETER

Altimeters are particularly useful in the following situations:

Ridges: if you are going up or down a well defined ridge, a compass bearing is unnecessary if you keep to the crest of the ridge. But it can be difficult in bad visibility to tell how far along the ridge you are. An accurate estimate of time will help, but an altimeter is more accurate and very simple to use.

Example: if you keep to the crest of the ridge, when the altimeter reads 780 metres you will be at point A.

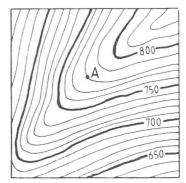

Fig. 40. Use of altimeter on a ridge.

Traversing. If traversing round a hill in bad visibility, there is a tendency to lose height; and if you are aware of this, you might over-correct the other way. An altimeter keeps you right.

Glaciers. An altimeter is invaluable on glaciers, especially when descending fast on skis. See the chapter 'Alpine Glacier Navigation'.

Many digital watches combine watch, alarm, and altimeter. The Suunto X-Lander also has a compass and the altimeter is calibrated to 5 metres. It is possible to be accurate to this degree.

Fig. 41 . A Suunto X-lander watch with altimeter.

Points to note in using an altimeter

1. Since it works off barometric pressure, the altimeter is affected by changes in the weather and it must, therefore, be continually adjusted by resetting it at known points. If you know, for example, that a trough of low pressure is coming through, be careful about this point.

2. For the same reason, if you go for more than 10 kilometres horizontal distance or for more than 500 vertical metres without resetting it, it may be inaccurate.

3. The speed at which you travel is important. If you are moving slowly, it could take 2 hours to cover 5 kilometres, and 2 hours is more than enough for pressure to change and for the instrument to be inaccurate,

4. The altimeter is affected by temperature changes. There is a complicated procedure for correcting this, but provided you reset regularly on known points, this can be (and in practice always is) ignored.

5. Method of use: if, for example, you are going from A at height 500 metres to B at height 800 metres, make sure that at A the altimeter is reading 500 metres. If it is not, adjust the setting so that it does. When you get to B it will read 800 metres. When at B a small adjustment due to barometric pressure or temperature may be necessary. Be sure to make this adjustment before continuing, because otherwise they become cumulative.

6. In the hut or tent you can use it overnight as a barometer, either by using the separate barometer on a digital watch or by setting the altimeter to the height of the hut. If in the morning the instrument shows the height of the hut to be higher than it actually is, the pressure has dropped. If it shows the height to be lower, the pressure has risen.

7. Some cheaper altimeters have calibrations every 50 metres or more, and these are useless for mountain navigation. 5 – 10 metres is recommended.

"MAP COVERS ARE LIKELY TO STRANGLE YOU !"

GPS - GLOBAL POSITIONING SYSTEM

A GPS receiver is an electronic device capable of calculating its position from satellites circling the earth. You can chose whether to have the position shown as a Latitude + Longitude or as a Grid Reference, and for mountaineering the latter is best - and your altitude is thrown in as well.

When you buy your GPS you will get an instruction book on how to set the device up. For Britain the co-ordinating system is OSGB, the Map Datum is GRB36, the Region is Europe and the Country is the UK. It's important to get these right and every time you go abroad, say to Switzerland or France, you need to change these set-up parameters, or the device will not work.

Fig. 42. Garmin GPS 60.

MAIN USES

The main uses of a GPS are:

1. To get a fix for where you are.
2. To take you to a specific point.
3. To follow a Route by taking you to a series of specific points one after the other.

1. To get a fix for where you are. The GPS gives you a grid reference, which in Britain starts with two letters e.g. NJ. These two letters identify the 100,000 metre square in which you are and they are printed in blue in the corner of the map. 8 figures then follow, 4 for the eastings and 4 for the northings, giving you a square 10 metres by 10 metres.

2. To take you to a specific point. These points are usually known as Waypoints - also Waymarks or Landmarks. First, on the map carefully work out the grid reference of the point to which you want to go; and then equally carefully enter this into your GPS as a Waypoint, giving it a name and following the instructions in the instruction book. All through this process there are opportunities for making mistakes, so do be careful and do check every step. Much greater accuracy will be obtained at the kitchen table before setting off, rather than on a windswept mountain with cold hands.

Press the GO TO button, select this Waypoint and the GPS will give you a bearing and distance. As you set off to the Waypoint, the GPS will continually update the bearing and distance.

3. To follow a Route.

The Route is like the GO TO button, except that it takes you to a number of Waypoints one after the other. For each Waypoint you need to work out the grid reference, enter it into the GPS and give it a name. From the Menu select Enter a Route, and you will now be asked to select the Waypoints in the order you wish to visit them. The GPS will then show each leg in turn, giving a bearing and distance to the next point; and it will automatically move onto the next leg without you having to touch any buttons.

Fig. 43. Skiing the route shown in Fig. 44.

Fig. 44 is a section of a Swiss map with 7 Waypoints marking a route which offers a fine ski descent in winter, but which, even in good weather, isn't exactly easy to follow. If you find the glades between the trees, you have a great ski run; but end up in the trees and you could have a dreadful time.

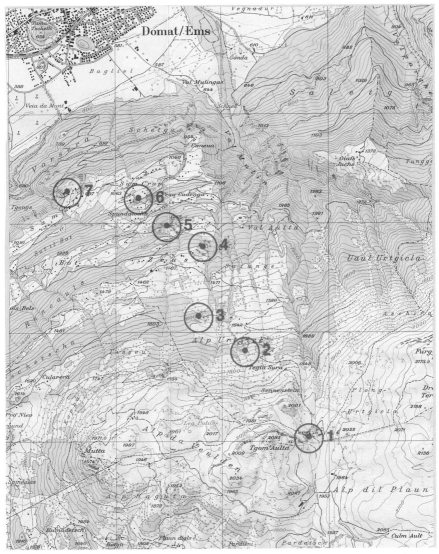

Fig. 44. A Route on a Swiss map.

You must get to the W side of the stream between points (2) and (3), as there is really no way down the E side.

(4) marks an important narrow section through the woods with a glade leading to (5).

Between (5) and (6) there are more open sections through the woods, and some houses.

And from (6) there is an open section to (7), where a track leads down to the valley.

DRAWBACKS OF GPS

1. There is a very real chance of entering data incorrectly. For example you may read a grid reference incorrectly off the map; even if that is correct, you may then enter it incorrectly on to the GPS; you may have the wrong Co-ordinating System or Map Datum entered; you may be following the wrong Waypoint.

2. The batteries may fail. If you use your GPS in cold winter weather, this is a very real issue.

3. As the weather deteriorates, so it becomes increasingly more difficult to see the screen and to operate the buttons with big gloves; until eventually you simply will not be able to use the device.

4. The GPS will not receive signals and therefore will not work in dense forest or when hemmed in by cliffs.

MORE ADVANCED USES OF A GPS

There are many computer programmes, which transfer data between a GPS receiver and a computer, and it depends how far you want to go.

Computer based map programmes. With a map on your computer all you have to do is click on a place and the programme automatically provides the co-ordinates. These are likely to be as a longitude/latitude, but when transferred the GPS will automatically convert them to grid references. It is the grid references which are transferred, not the map - that stays on the computer.

Maps downloadable to a GPS. If your GPS is capable of storing downloadable maps, you can do everything on your GPS screen: select your waypoints and routes, and watch the whole thing unfurl on the screen.

These more advanced uses are outside the scope of this book, but if you are interested in this aspect of GPS I recommend *"Getting To Grips With GPS"* by Peter Judd and Simon Brown, published by Cordee UK.

CONCLUSION

A GPS is a great tool, I often use one and they are good fun to play with. But I know that the batteries will fail someday and that physically I cannot use it in very bad weather conditions - and for the foreseeable generations of GPS, these points will still apply. So I always use it in conjunction with a map, a compass and an altimeter; and I am always aware of the contour lines, which I believe are the single most important tool in navigation.

BAD WEATHER NAVIGATION

When the weather is fine, particularly when the visibility is clear, navigation can be done quickly and effectively by map reading alone. But in conditions of bad weather, the other skills (compass, estimating time and paces, altimeter and GPS) are very necessary, and at any one time you probably use a selection of those techniques. In addition to what has already been said about those skills, there are one or two other factors which can help navigation in bad conditions.

1. Preparation.   Time spent at home, in the hut or in the tent looking at the map and the intended route is time very well spent. Take note of any escape routes which could be useful if the weather were to get really bad.

2. Route Card. The classic route card contains, for every leg of the intended trip: grid reference of the departure and arrival points, description of route, distance, vertical height gain or loss, compass bearing, and estimated time. As a classroom exercise it is useful enough, but as an aid to actual navigation on the mountain, it can, in my view, be a dangerous thing, since you will feel constrained to follow this route which you prepared by the warmth of the fire at home, while other factors (like the fitness of the party, weather conditions or conditions underfoot) indicate a change of plan.

Anything which constrains your judgement on the mountain is dangerous - be it a rigid plan to meet friends at a particular place or a route card or anything else.

So a route card should be short, if at all. It might consist of just one vital bearing, so that you don't have to fight on a windy col to take it off the map.

3. Access to map and compass.
* Have a jacket with a proper map pocket.
* Buy a map which is waterproofed; or cover it with a waterproof cover yourself; or keep it in a polybag.
* Keep the compass on the zipper of your map pocket; or, if you prefer to keep it round your neck, make sure the loop is long enough so that you can use it with the map.

- Avoid map cases, which are fine in good weather, but are likely to strangle you in strong wind.
- Write any timing charts and pacing formulas as aide-memoires on the back of the map.

4. Back marker. In a group of four or more people, ask someone to bring up the back, preferably someone responsible and in easily recognisable clothing.

5. Navigation checker. In conditions of white-out or other bad visibility, it is very difficult to follow a compass bearing accurately. Quite a good system is to ask someone else to walk in your steps about 10 metres behind, depending on conditions, and to ask a third person to walk the same distance again behind the second person. This third person will have a compass with the bearing, and will find it fairly easy to sight through the second person to you and to see whether or not you are keeping on course. Every now and again you can look back, and the third person can indicate to you how you are doing.

This system is infinitely preferable to the man-out-in-front system, whereby you send someone else in front and give them directions from behind, because:

i   if you are the most experienced person, you should be out in front, particularly in winter when you might have dangerous cornices or avalanches slopes.
ii. by briefing your checker to indicate to you only when you look back allows steady progress to be made without too many stops.
iii. the man-out-in-front system usually results in shouting, misunderstandings and a fair amount of stop-go.

6. Aiming-off.

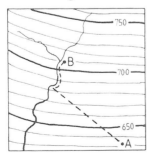

In the example you are going from A to the stream junction at B. If you take a direct bearing, you might miss it and not know on which side you missed it. By deliberating aiming-off to below the junction and then following the stream up to it, you are sure of success.

Fig. 45. Aiming-off.

7. Attack points. Orienteers use attack points as a matter of course and this technique can be used effectively in mountain navigation. Identify on the map the point to which you are heading. If this is indistinct, pick out a more distinct point nearby - one which will be clearly identifiable once you get there and one which is easy enough to reach. This is the attack point. Navigate to the attack point and then go on to your point. If you fail to find your point, return to the attack point and try again.

8. Rope-up. If there is a risk of falling over crags, cliffs or into crevasses put the rope on in plenty of time. If you are traversing round the headwall of a corrie or cwm, the navigator will want to be as close to the headwall as possible, as it is a good feature by which to navigate. In winter there may well be a dangerous cornice to watch for. The danger is that, if the navigator falls over the edge, the rest might be dragged over too. To avoid this happening, rope as shown in Fig. 46.

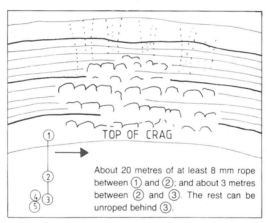

Fig. 46. Roping-up when parallel to steep ground.

9. Traverses. Bear in mind that on a traverse there is a tendency to lose height.

10. Steady pace. Keep a steady pace, because:
- Continuity of speed helps calculate estimates of time.
- In a group, a short pause by the leader results in a much longer wait by the people at the back.
- Continual stops generate a feeling of mistrust in the navigator - does this person know what they're doing ?

11. Concentration. Serious navigation requires concentration, so don't allow people to stray in front of you or to the side, as they will pull you off course.

12. High wind. Keep off exposed ridges and try to use the natural shapes of the landscape for protection.
- Wind accelerates up slopes and decelerates down them.
- If approaching the headwall of a corrie and you are heading into the wind, there will probably be a calm spot about 15 metres before the headwall.
- It may be necessary to rope-up.
- It is safe enough to exert yourself against a strong wind if at any time you can turn round and retreat safely with the wind behind you - while the converse is not true.
- A strong side wind blows you off course, so remember to adjust accordingly by deliberately walking into the wind.

13. Deep snow. The easiest going will be on the ridges and windward slopes; while the worst will be in the hollows and on lee slopes.

14. Avalanches. A safe route will depend on recognising avalanche conditions, but this is big subject and is outside the scope of this book. As far as Britain is concerned, our most usual avalanche is the windslab, which forms on lee slopes. Identifying windslab can be very difficult, as local features cause wind eddies, which put windslab down on the most unexpected places - even on windward slopes. By keeping to ridges and windward slopes, the danger will be greatly reduced.

15. Sudden mist or cloud. If the mist or cloud suddenly comes in:
- Take a compass bearing on the next point before it disappears.
- If you are in any doubt as to where you are, try and get a fix before being enveloped.
- Get the party together.
- Small features in mist may look bigger than they actually are. For example, a small knoll 10 metres high (which may not be on the map) can loom up in the mist and look like something 50 – 60 metres high; and this can be misleading.

16. White-out. This is a snow condition of appalling visibility where it is impossible to distinguish between the horizon and the ground; where it is not possible to tell what is, say, 3 metres in front of you. There could be a vertical drop, flat ground or a hill - and you simply cannot see it. This may occur in conditions of high wind and driving snow, i.e. a blizzard; but it may equally well occur in very still conditions. Anyone going out regularly in snow conditions will come across this condition, and the following points will help:

- In order to get some feedback as to what is in front or to the sides, throw snowballs - 7 to 10 metres will be enough. While this obviously does not work too well in a blizzard, it is of great practical help in still conditions.
- Ask people to walk on either side of you. This will give useful feedback, particularly if you are in a group large enough to spare two or three people on either side. A situation where this works well is where you are following a broad ridge, and in a white-out it is easy to wander off the crest; but with people out on the sides you will see what is happening: if you are on the crest, they should be below you.
- White-out is broken up by features such as rocks and human beings. Look carefully for cairns which may mark paths, path junctions or tops of hills.
- Use small features which would normally be ignored. For example, 2 contour lines close together on an otherwise uniform slope indicate a short steep bit. This is definitely useable, although on a nice sunny day it would not even be noticed. Use the compass plus estimate of time and paces to reach it, and then move on to the next feature.
- Consider what you have been doing and plot that on the map. For example, you may know just two things: firstly, that for the last 10 or 15 minutes you have been walking on flat ground; and, secondly, the bearing. Put that bearing (converted to grid) on the map and move it around the area you think you are in. Where one long edge of the compass crosses flat ground will, probably, be the flat ground you have just crossed.
- Drawing an analogy from yacht navigation, a position may be an E.P. (Estimated Position) or a Fix. The latter is where there is no doubt at all that your position is correct; and the E.P. is where there is doubt. From a Fix you can head off in confidence; while from the E.P. you head off with less confidence, looking for the first opportunity to get a Fix or another E.P. , and constantly aware that you may not have been where the first E.P. put you.

However, the E.P. is a vital step and should not be ignored just because it is a bit woolly. They build up a picture as to where you are and they enable you to work your way along until you get a fix.

17. Precision v. judgement. Navigation is seldom a very precise exercise and is more about carefully assessing the information you have to hand. Two mistakes which are made fairly regularly are:
- Expecting everything to be crystal clear all the time.
- Ignoring information which is at hand - e.g. the type of ground you have been walking over for the last 30 minutes. The mistake is in failing to recognise that this information could be put to good use, and in then failing to assess it's particular use correctly.

18. Searching for a point. Where a group is approaching a point in bad visibility, the standard sweep search is useful. All you do is, instead of walking bunched up, spread out in a line abreast, so as to maximise the chance of finding the point. Fig 47 shows a group of 5 people walking on a bearing AB, sweep searching for Point P.

Fig. 47. Sweep search.

Since someone on their own cannot by definition do a sweep search, a box search is useful in that situation. Referring to Fig. 48 presume that you are on a bearing AB looking for Point P. You could be anywhere along the line AB, but the time comes when you decide to start searching.

Walk N for 10 paces; walk E for 10 paces; walk W for 20 paces; walk N for 30 paces; and continue this pattern until the point is found.

Fig. 48. Box search by solo walker.

ALPINE GLACIER NAVIGATION

To navigate safely on glaciers and big Alpine snowfields obviously requires knowledge of snow, glaciers and avalanches - a subject which is outside the scope of this book.

DIFFERENCES BETWEEN BRITISH AND CONTINENTAL MAPS

1. Shading. If you open a Swiss map (Carte Nationale de la Suisse) or an Austrian map (Alpenverienskarte), you will probably be impressed by the three dimensional effect. The map is almost a photograph, with the ridges and glaciers very obvious.

Much of this is due to shading. For example, the Swiss maps have the slopes facing north and west shaded lighter than those facing south and east.

2. Grid Lines. Some maps have few grid lines and others use a different numbering system.

3. Magnetic Variation. This is less than in Britain and for practical purposes is ignored.

4. Ski Routes. For the main areas you have a choice between a map with ski routes and one without. The ski routes are recommended routes for winter and spring tourers, and on the back of some maps, e.g. the Swiss 1:50,000, are short route descriptions in guidebook form, giving approximate times.

ACCURACY OF GLACIER INFORMATION

A glacier is a moving river of ice, continually being fed from the top and sides while melting at the bottom. All the time it is moving downhill due to gravity, so that, if you fall into a crevasse at the top of a glacier, you will eventually come out at the bottom.

If the balance between feeding and melting is equal, the glacier keeps its shape. If the balance is unequal, the glacier will be either advancing or retreating. If the glacier you are on is not stable and if the survey was last done several years ago (as is often the case), you may have some problems, for example:

- The snout or end of the glacier may be a long way further back than indicated on the map, easily as much as 200 vertical metres or one kilometre horizontally.

- A guidebook may advise a summer route which goes up the glacier for a while and then takes to the rocks at the side. If the glacier has retreated, the rocks which have subsequently been exposed may be extremely smooth and difficult to climb; and your 'easy glacier route' starts to take on different dimensions.

*"IT WASN'T LIKE THIS WHEN I CAME WITH
YOUR GRANDFATHER 40 YEARS AGO !".*

- A hut which was once built by the side of the glacier may now be left perched well above it, like the Konkordia Hut in the Bernese Oberland, which has a long section of ladder leading up to it.

- Crevasses which are marked on the map may not be there; and more important, a glacier which is marked as being crevasse free may become heavily crevassed. A year or two later they may have gone.

PLANNING A ROUTE

1. To avoid some of the problems just mentioned, take local advice - e.g. hut guardians and mountain guides. It helps greatly if you speak their language, even if they speak English.

2. Having taken the advice, it is usually necessary to interpret it for your own needs. It seems to me that advice tends to err on the safe side and if your party is strong, you may wish to bear that in mind.

3. Plan to avoid the sides of glaciers where possible as there are more crevasses there. There is also the danger of stonefalls and avalanches from the slopes above.

4. Plan to move from one identifiable point to another - e.g. rocks, ridges, huts, ends of glaciers etc.

PRACTICAL POINTS

1. Identifiable points. Having planned to keep to the middle of the glacier to avoid crevasses, stonefalls and avalanches, you may find in bad visibility that you have to go to the side in order to pick up an identifiable point, like a rock ridge coming down to the glacier.

2. Straight lines. If you keep to as straight a line as possible and make turns as open as possible (particularly on skis), this will make life easier for the people following - and for yourself if you return this way.

3. Avalanche debris. Debris from snow and ice avalanches sometimes lies across the intended route. Identify the debris as to ice or snow, and then look to see where it has come from. It may be snow, or it may be ice from a fallen serac. The snow debris may well be frozen into awkward lumps, and the ice will certainly be difficult to cross. Cross quickly and avoid making a turn; and if there is a danger of a further avalanche and if it looks as though the crossing of the debris will take a long time, an alternative route might well be advised.

Often snow debris indicates safety, on the argument that the avalanche has brought down all the unstable snow and that the remaining snow is stable.

On the other hand, if a fallen serac has scattered lumps of ice across your path, it is likely that any remaining seracs will do the same.

4. Potential avalanche slopes. Inevitably these sometimes have to be crossed. Cross fast, one at a time; avoid a traverse line if possible; and try to avoid turning skis near them. Those on safe ground should watch those crossing in case they are avalanched.

5. Crevasses. Expect to find them where the ice is under tension - e.g. on the inside of bends, where rock ridges extend into the glacier, and where the glacier falls more steeply.

If in bad visibility you come across a crevasse in front of you:

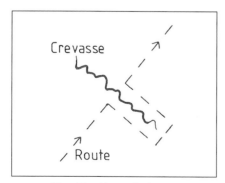

- Move off at right angles to the compass course until you find a safe crossing point.
- Measure this distance approximately by rope lengths.
- After crossing the crevasse, move back the same distance on the other side and resume the compass course.

Fig.49. Negotiating a crevasse in bad visibility.

6. Altimeter. This is an invaluable instrument when ascending or descending glaciers, particularly when skiing down them as you lose height very quickly, and if you are not careful you can find that you have gone too far in the wrong direction and have to climb back up.

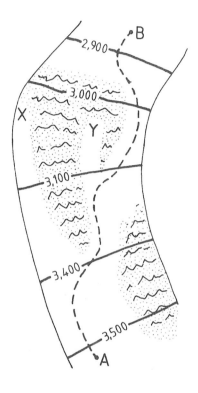

Fig. 50. Use of an altimeter on a glacier.

In the example Fig.50 in order to ski down from A to B, you would take the dotted line.

At first this keeps to the left of centre in order to avoid the crevasses on the right. At 3,400 metres it moves to the right and failure to do so would mean you ended up at point **X**, with a climb back out.

At 3,100 metres you have to cross over to the right, to avoid ending up at point **Y**.

At 3,000 metres start moving back out to the centre of the glacier, as this is usually the safest place to be, reaching it at 2,900 metres.

An altimeter is invaluable for making the turns.

Remember: what took 5 minutes to descend could take an hour to re-ascend. Add the time to get out of a crevasse, and you could spend the night there.

7. Descent route. If planning to come back down the same way:

Note carefully the position of crevasses while ascending the glacier.

While descending, keep close to the uphill track if it hasn't been blown in or unless the snow conditions dictate otherwise. For example, north facing slopes will hold powder snow longer in the day than south facing ones, and the skier will look for powder. A small depression or ridge off to one side of the climbing track may offer better conditions later in the day.

IF LOST ....

Let us think of two stages of 'being lost'. The really bad one is where you don't even know which mountain you are on, and in this case I can offer the following advice: work your way slowly downhill following streams, as these tend to lead eventually to habitation; and before you go out again on the hill, maybe read this book again and buy a GPS.

But normally, when we say we are lost, what we mean is that, temporarily, we are not sure exactly where we are. We know which mountain we are on, but not exactly whereabouts on it. Maybe something unexpected has appeared out of the gloom.

MAYBE SOMETHING UNEXPECTED HAS
APPEARED OUT OF THE GLOOM ....

1. Sit down and think back to what you have been doing:

*   What type of terrain have you been walking on ? Was it flat, up or down ?
*   In what direction were you walking ? Did you have a bearing ?
*   For how long were you walking in that direction ? If you know the time, you can work out the distance.

2. Take an aspect of slope.

These two stages should give you an estimated position (an E.P.), and the next step is to try and confirm this to a definite position (a Fix) by moving off and getting new data. Normally it is easiest to make gentle descending traverses, but the direction in which you actually go depends entirely on the terrain on which you find yourself.

For example:

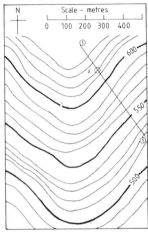

After the 'Sit and Think' and the aspect of slope, you think you are possibly somewhere near the line marked (1), maybe near point **X**.

This is very much a guess, but the best you can come up with in the circumstances.

Fig. 51.

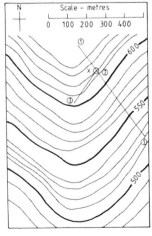

To get more data, you move off, in this case in a gently descending traverse (line 2).

You take a bearing, in this case about 216° grid.

And you go for a measured distance , done by timing and pacing - in this case 200 metres.

Fig. 52.

59

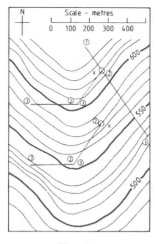

Fig. 53.

When you get to the end of that leg, take stock again:
• What is the terrain ?
• What is the aspect of slope ?

Does this new information fit in with where you find yourself ?

Then move off on another leg in order to get yet more data (line 3).

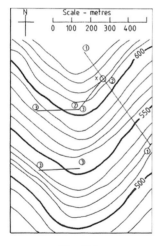

Fig. 54.

At the end of this leg (i.e. at the end of line 3), take stock again:
• What is the terrain ?
• What is the aspect of slope ?

Does it fit ?

Assume in the example that, as you came to the end of this leg (line 3), the ground steepened. If we were where we thought we might be, the gradient would be constant. But if you look further down the map, there are some contour lines closer together, on a slope with the same aspect.

So, if we are there, work line 3 back from that position, to see where it started. And that fits, according to the aspect of slope.

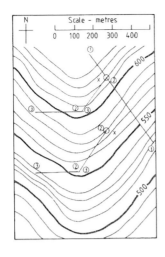

Then work line 2 back on the map, and see if that fits.

In this case it does, as the start of both line 2's are on the same aspect of slope.

Fig. 55.

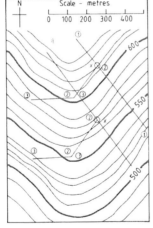

Then plot line 1 on the map and see if that fits. In this case it does.

So the original Estimated Position at point **X** was in the wrong position - it should have been lower down.

Fig. 56.

Conclusion. There are two types of data available: that which is already available at the point we think we are lost, and the data we can get by moving off on short legs - there is a tendency to ignore both. Also, it is tempting to make the data fit the situation (one of the big mistakes regularly made in mountain navigation) - so try to remain analytical and open-minded. Finally, taking the aspect of the slope is an invaluable technique.

THE AUTHOR

Peter Cliff is an International Mountain Guide.

He was born in Crayke, York; and education included Southampton University (Law Degree) and Bangor University (Certificate of Education).

His first work as a professional mountaineer and teacher of sailing was with the Outward Bound Schools, followed by 20 years on the Cairngorm Mountains of Scotland during which he was for 10 years leader of the Cairngorm Mountain Rescue Team.

As a Mountain Guide he has worked in most areas of the Alps and as a Yachtmaster he has sailed off the West Coast of Scotland, the Faroe Island, the North Sea, France, Greece, Turkey and a crossing of the Indian Ocean.

His other books are "A Guidebook to the Haute Route", "Alpinism" and "Ski Mountaineering".

Peter Cliff, Mosswood Cottage, Crayke, York YO61 4TQ.
Email: peter@skisafaris.co.uk
Website: www.skisafaris.co.uk